Instant PrimeFaces Starter

Design and develop awesome web user interfaces for desktop and mobile devices with PrimeFaces and JSF2 using practical, hands-on examples

Ian Hlavats

BIRMINGHAM - MUMBAI

Instant PrimeFaces Starter

First published: June 2013

Production Reference: 1200613

Published by Packt Publishing Ltd.
Livery Place
35 Livery Street
Birmingham B3 2PB, UK.

ISBN 978-1-84951-990-8

www.packtpub.com

Credits

Author

Ian Hlavats

Reviewers

Daniel Hinojosa

Kito D. Mann

David Stasuik

Acquisition Editor

Edward Gordon

Commissioning Editor

Harsha Bharwani

Technical Editors

Dennis John

Pragati Singh

Project Coordinator

Amigya Khurana

Proofreader

Lawrence A. Herman

Production Coordinator

Nilesh R. Mohite

Cover Work

Nilesh R. Mohite

Cover Image

Abhinash Sahu

Foreword

I created PrimeFaces to make it easy to add rich UI components to JSF applications. Today, PrimeFaces has become a mature and powerful library with over 100 flexible and easy-to-use UI components, built-in Ajax, theme awareness, HTML5 support, mobile optimized rendering, and much more. PrimeFaces has been adopted by many companies and organizations, and has a strong and helpful community of users.

Ian has been an important member of the PrimeFaces community for some time. I first met him at JSF Summit in Orlando, in 2009 where he was giving talks on JSF development and promoting his first book, *JSF 1.2 Components*. He wrote about PrimeFaces in his first book, and I am glad he was able to give it a complete coverage in this title. Since that conference, Ian and I have become friends, and he has demonstrated a true commitment to the JSF community and ecosystem.

He has given the official PrimeFaces talk at JAXConf in San Jose and San Francisco for the past couple of years, and he developed a Dreamweaver extension for PrimeFaces. I worked with Ian on the JSF 2.2 Expert Group this year, and I know you are in good hands while reading this book.

Çağatay Çivici,

Creator of PrimeFaces

About the Author

Ian Hlavats is an experienced Java developer, instructor, speaker, and author of the book JSF 1.2 Components (Packt). He has worked for clients in government, insurance, and entertainment industries, writing Java applications using Swing, Struts, JSF2, PrimeFaces, jQuery, and other UI technologies. He has delivered Java courses in college and corporate training environments including a one-year engagement with Cognos/IBM.

He is on the JSF 2.2 Expert Group and contributed to the next generation of the JSF specification. A regular speaker at Java EE conferences, he has given presentations on JSF and PrimeFaces technologies since 2008 at JSF Summit, NFJS, and JAXConf in San Francisco. He is the creator of JSFToolbox for Dreamweaver, a suite of design and coding extensions for JSF developers. He co-hosts a podcast on JSF and Java EE technologies with fellow authors Kito D. Mann and Daniel Hinojosa. He holds a Bachelor of Humanities degree from Carleton University and IT certificates from Algonquin College.

I would like to thank my colleagues Kito D. Mann and Daniel Hinojosa for their camaraderie and support, my friend Phil Stang for his insight and guidance, my wife for her understanding and patience, and my excellent publishing team including Amigya Khurana and Harsha Bharwani for their diligence and commitment to excellence in this project.

About the Reviewers

Daniel Hinojosa has been teaching, speaking, and programming for private, educational, and government entities since the dawning of the new century. Some like to call this time period 1999. His business encompasses a torrent of titillating technologies such as Scala, JBoss Seam and Application Server, Guice, Spring, Groovy, and more. He is co-founder of the Albuquerque Java User's Group. He is also co-host of the Enterprise Java Newscast, formerly called the JSF and JavaEE Newscast. He also an author of Testing in Scala.

Kito D. Mann is the Principal Consultant at Virtua Inc., specializing in enterprise application architecture, training, development, and mentoring with JavaServer Faces, portlets, Liferay, and Java EE technologies. He is also the editor-in-chief of JSFCentral.com (`www.jsfcentral.com`), co-host of the Enterprise Java Newscast (`http://blogs.jsfcentral.com/JSFNewscast/category/Newscasts`), host of the JSF Podcast interview series (`http://www.jsfcentral.com/resources/jsfcentralpodcasts/`), and the author of JavaServer Faces in Action (Manning). He has participated in several Java Community Process expert groups (including JSF and Portlets) and is also an internationally recognized speaker. He holds a BA in Computer Science from Johns Hopkins University.

David Stasuik has spent nearly 16 years in the software industry working with both the private and public sectors. The majority of his career has been in Java-based environments dealing with both desktop and web-based applications.

He started out as a developer and worked his way up through technical and development management roles. He now works as an architect/senior developer for the Canadian government. In addition, he is currently consulting with a private company as an architect and senior developer in the creation of a high volume web-based application based on JSF 2.0 that implements the PrimeFaces JSF components.

When not immersed in work and technology, he spends his downtime pursing his passion for reading and sports and also spends time with his wife and two children.

www.packtpub.com

Support files, eBooks, discount offers and more

You might want to visit www.packtpub.com for support files and downloads related to your book.

Did you know that Packt offers eBook versions of every book published, with PDF and ePub files available? You can upgrade to the eBook version at www.packtpub.com and, as a print book customer, you are entitled to a discount on the eBook copy. Get in touch with us at service@packtpub.com for more details.

At www.packtpub.com, you can also read a collection of free technical articles, sign up for a range of free newsletters, and receive exclusive discounts and offers on Packt Publishing books and eBooks.

packtlib.packtpub.com

Do you need instant solutions to your IT questions? PacktLib is Packt's online digital book library. Here, you can access, read, and search across Packt's entire library of books.

Why Subscribe?

+ Fully searchable across every book published by Packt Publishing
+ Copy and paste, print, and bookmark content
+ On demand and accessible via web browser

Free Access for Packt account holders

If you have an account with Packt at www.packtpub.com, you can use this to access PacktLib today and view nine entirely free books. Simply use your login credentials for immediate access.

Table of Contents

Instant PrimeFaces Starter

Welcome to the *Instant PrimeFaces Starter*. This book has been especially created to provide you with all the information that you need to get up to speed with PrimeFaces—the next generation JSF component toolkit. You will learn the basics of PrimeFaces, get started with building your first PrimeFaces application, learn about the key concepts in the PrimeFaces library, PrimeFaces Ajax components, writing mobile applications with PrimeFaces, and using Prime Push to build multicast-style web applications such as chat rooms or auction systems.

This document contains the following sections:

So, what is PrimeFaces? will explain about the PrimeFaces library, what makes it great, and how to use it to build real-world web and mobile applications.

Installation will help you learn how to download, install, and configure PrimeFaces in your web application so you can begin using it immediately.

Quick start – Implementing a sample project using PrimeFaces will show you how to design and implement a web user interface based on the PrimeFaces UI toolkit. It also lists the steps to create a basic web application with PrimeFaces that can be used as the basis for more complex real-world projects in the future.

Top 3 features you need to know about will help provide an in-depth functional overview of PrimeFaces and serves as a development guide for the top PrimeFaces components and features: PrimeFaces UI components, PrimeFaces Mobile, and Prime Push.

People and places you should get to know lists a number of tools and resources available to support your learning process. Since every open source project is centered around a community, you will find many supportive users and useful information to help you build PrimeFaces applications quickly and professionally.

So, what is PrimeFaces?

PrimeFaces is one of the coolest technologies available today for developing web applications with **JavaServer Faces** (**JSF**). Simply put, it has never been easier to build powerful, rich, and functional web applications for desktop and mobile browsers than it is today. This is due to the awe-inspiring ingenuity of PrimeFaces, and the excellent engineering that has gone into the design, implementation, and evolution of this amazing open source technology.

When I first met Çağatay Çivici, the founder of PrimeFaces, at the JSF Summit conference in Orlando, Florida in 2009, I was most impressed with how calmly and coolly he delivered his talk on PrimeFaces components.

In attendance in the conference room were senior developers, architects, and technical leads from JBoss, ICEsoft, and Sun Microsystems; each competing to develop the best Ajax-enabled UI components to drive evolution forward in the JSF ecosystem. As he spoke about one slide after another, the level of astonishment in the room kept rising. He showed us data tables, grids, trees, and rich input components with effects, drag-and-drop, and seemingly effortless Ajax.

With each example, the ingenuity and creativity of this technology became clearer and clearer. It peaked with a demonstration of a mock Mac OS X operating system built entirely for the Web, featuring a desktop background, dock toolbar, Growl-like messages, and a console with a command-line interface. If that wasn't enough, what followed was a demonstration of a mobile UI toolkit for JSF that enables developers to write mobile web applications with minimal code.

At this point it became clear to me that PrimeFaces was the most advanced UI component library in the JSF space in terms of creative vision, design, and implementation. Indeed, PrimeFaces has accomplished something great. PrimeFaces makes it fun and easy to design and build sophisticated web applications for a Web 2.0 world with JSF2, Java EE, and the latest technologies such as jQuery, HTML5, WebSockets, and Ajax.

So what is PrimeFaces? If you have worked with other JSF technologies such as JBoss RichFaces, and ICEfaces from ICEsoft Technologies, or Apache MyFaces Trinidad; you'll already be familiar with the concepts you need to understand to get up to speed quickly with PrimeFaces. Like these other libraries, PrimeFaces includes a wide range of Ajax-enabled UI components such as layout panels, charts, buttons, links, data tables, grids, calendars, modal dialogs, and more with support for themes, effects, jQuery, drag-and-drop, and the much-improved JSF2 API.

PrimeFaces provides an arsenal of feature-rich UI components with a high degree of usability, sophistication, flexibility, and interactivity. These features make PrimeFaces a powerful technology for JSF developers that offer significant advantages over the standard JSF components.

Another great feature of PrimeFaces is the **PrimeFaces Mobile UI toolkit**. Designing and building mobile applications that work consistently across devices is a challenge faced by developers today.

There are generally the following three approaches to writing mobile applications that target multiple devices today:

✦ Writing the application natively using the mobile platform's SDK

✦ Writing a web application that has the same look and feel as the mobile platform and is accessed from a web browser on the device

✦ Writing a hybrid application with a native mobile user interface that contains a browser window for interacting with a web application

PrimeFaces Mobile implements the second approach and provides a set of JSF tags that render UI components using the mobile platform's look and feel. The supported platforms include iOS, Android, BlackBerry, Windows Phone, MeeGo, and others. PrimeFaces Mobile extends all the benefits of the JSF API to mobile devices and makes it easy for developers to build data-intensive mobile applications using a familiar programming model and application architecture.

PrimeFaces also includes **PrimePush**, an Ajax Push servlet based on the Atmosphere framework and similar to ICEfaces' Ajax Push. Ajax Push is useful for building multicast-style web applications where a server-side event can be broadcasted to multiple clients, such as desktop and mobile users, at the same time.

This book will help you to understand quickly how PrimeFaces works, and will get you up to speed on how to use PrimeFaces in your JSF applications. It will also teach you how to use PrimePush and PrimeFaces Mobile to build truly outstanding web applications for desktop and mobile users.

By the end of this book, you will have a good understanding of PrimeFaces, and I hope you will be able to see for yourself why PrimeFaces is one of today's most popular JSF component libraries, trusted by companies such as Boeing, Ford, Cisco, Nvidia, Western Union, Verizon, Costco, and many others.(For Windows users, you can install the GitHub client at `http://windows.github.com`. For Mac users, please visit `http://mac.github.com`.)

Installation

PrimeFaces is a lightweight library with minimal external dependencies and zero configuration. It is possible to add PrimeFaces to a JSF2 application by copying a single JAR file! We want to demonstrate all the capabilities of PrimeFaces, so we will take a few moments to set up our development environment before we take a deep dive into PrimeFaces. We will use Eclipse 4 (Juno) with Maven support as our Java IDE, GlassFish 3 as our Java EE 6 application server, and Adobe Dreamweaver CS6 with JSF, Facelets, and PrimeFaces plugins as our web authoring tool.

Step 1 – Installing Eclipse

If you don't already have Eclipse installed, please take a moment to download Eclipse for Java EE Developers from `www.eclipse.org`. Once you have Eclipse installed, we will add a couple of Eclipse plugins to simplify the development process.

Installing Eclipse Marketplace

Eclipse introduced a great feature called the **Eclipse Marketplace** that allows easy installation of plugins to customize the IDE. We will use the Eclipse Marketplace to install additional plugins to simplify development. So let's make sure this feature is installed. If you see the **Eclipse Marketplace** menu item under the **Help** menu, you already have the Eclipse Marketplace client installed; otherwise perform the following steps:

1. Navigate to **Help | Install New Software**.
2. Select **All Available Sites** in the **Work With** field.
3. Type `Marketplace Client` in the search field.
4. Install the `Marketplace Client` plugin from under **General Purpose Tools**.

Step 2 – Installing Maven

Maven is a widely used project configuration and dependency management tool for Java. We will use it throughout this book to configure and build the example project in a consistent way. PrimeFaces provides a Maven repository that makes it easy to download and install the necessary JAR files.

To install the m2eclipse plugin, perform the following steps:

1. Launch Eclipse and navigate to **Help | Eclipse Marketplace**.
2. Type `maven` and click on the **Go** button to search for the **m2eclipse** plugin, and then click on the **Install** button.
3. Restart Eclipse when prompted.

Next, we will install the **Maven Integration for WTP** plugin for Eclipse. This plugin enables us to deploy a Maven project to an application server managed using the Eclipse **Web Tools Platform** (**WTP**).

To install the plugin perform the following steps:

1. Navigate to **Help | Eclipse Marketplace** again and search for m2eclipse-wtp.
2. Install the plugin and restart Eclipse.

Step 3 – Installing GlassFish

GlassFish is an open source Java EE 6 application server that ships with the **Mojarra** JSF2 reference implementation. PrimeFaces requires JSF2, so GlassFish is a good choice for our environment. We could also use Tomcat 7, JBoss AS 7, or other Java EE 6 compliant application servers.

We will use the **Servers** view in Eclipse to install the GlassFish server connector. To install, perform the following steps:

1. Click on the **Servers** tab.
2. Click on the **new server wizard** link.
3. Then click on the **download additional server adapters** link and wait for the list to populate.
4. Select **Oracle GlassFish Server Tools** and click on **Next**.
5. Accept the license agreement, click on **Finish**, and then click on **OK**.
6. When Eclipse has finished installing the connector, click on **Yes** to restart the workbench.
7. When Eclipse restarts, once again click on the **Servers** tab and click on the **new server wizard** link. Run it.

    You should now see **GlassFish** listed in the available server connectors.

8. Select a recent version of GlassFish and click on **Next**.
9. Select a JRE and enter a path for the GlassFish installation directory, for example, your user home directory.
10. Click on **Install Server** and wait for Eclipse to download and install GlassFish 3.
11. When GlassFish is installed, click on **Finish** to close the wizard.

Step 4 – Installing Dreamweaver

We will be using Adobe Dreamweaver CS6 with JSF plugins as our web-authoring tool for the examples in this book. You can download a 30-day trial version of Dreamweaver from www.adobe.com.

You can also download JSFToolbox for Dreamweaver from my website, www.jsftoolbox.com. This is a suite of design and coding extensions I created that adds support for JSF2, Facelets, and PrimeFaces development to Dreamweaver. As a long-time Dreamweaver user, I wanted to use JSF components in Dreamweaver, so I wrote these extensions and used them for UI development in all my JSF projects. JSFToolbox for Dreamweaver is also available as a 30-day trial.

Step 5 – Installing MySQL

The sample application in this book uses the MySQL database. You can download and install the MySQL database server for your operating system from www.mysql.com. The application uses Hibernate to create the database schema on startup, but requires you to create the database and grant permissions before running the app. Please run the following commands with the mysql command line tool:

1. `mysql -u root -p`

2. Type in the root password you chose during installation and press enter. The mysql command prompt will appear.

3. `mysql> create database mycompany;`

4. `mysql> grant all on mycompany.* to 'user'@'localhost' identified by 'user';`

Step 6 – Installing PrimeFaces

Now that we have set up our development environment, we are ready to create our first PrimeFaces project! The steps to create a new Eclipse project with PrimeFaces and Maven support are simple:

1. In Eclipse, navigate to **File** | **New** | **Other** | **Maven** | **Maven Project**.

2. Check the **Create a simple project** checkbox and click on **Next**.

3. Enter com.mycompany for the group ID and primefaces-starter for the artifact ID.

4. Change the packaging type to war and click on **Finish**.

Now, we will add the PrimeFaces Maven repository and dependencies to the Maven pom.xml configuration file for our project. The relevant Maven configuration for PrimeFaces is shown in the following code snippet:

```
<project xmlns="http://maven.apache.org/POM/4.0.0" xmlns:xsi="http://
www.w3.org/2001/XMLSchema-instance"
xsi:schemaLocation="http://maven.apache.org/POM/4.0.0 http://maven.
apache.org/xsd/maven-4.0.0.xsd">
<modelVersion>4.0.0</modelVersion>
<groupId>com.mycompany</groupId>
<artifactId>primefaces-webapp</artifactId>
<version>0.0.1-SNAPSHOT</version>
```

```xml
<packaging>war</packaging>
<repositories>
<repository>
<id>prime-repo</id>
<name>PrimeFaces Maven Repository</name>
<url>http://repository.primefaces.org</url>
<layout>default</layout>
</repository>
<repository>
<id>codehaus-snapshots</id>
<url>http://snapshots.repository.codehaus.org</url>
</repository>
<repository>
<id>jboss-public-repository-group</id>
<name>JBoss Public Maven Repository Group</name>
<url>https://repository.jboss.org/nexus/content/groups/
public-jboss/</url>
<layout>default</layout>
</repository>
</repositories>
<dependencies>

<!-- PrimeFaces -->
<dependency>
<groupId>org.primefaces</groupId>
<artifactId>primefaces</artifactId>
<version>3.5</version>
</dependency>
<dependency>
<groupId>org.primefaces</groupId>
<artifactId>primefaces-mobile</artifactId>
<version>1.0.0-SNAPSHOT</version>
</dependency>
<dependency>
<groupId>org.glassfish</groupId>
<artifactId>javax.faces</artifactId>
<version>2.1.10</version>
</dependency>

<!-- PrimeFaces Push -->
<!-- Atmosphere -->
<dependency>
<groupId>org.atmosphere</groupId>
<artifactId>atmosphere-runtime</artifactId>
<version>1.0.10</version>
<exclusions>
<exclusion>
```

```xml
<artifactId>slf4j-api</artifactId>
<groupId>org.slf4j</groupId>
</exclusion>
</exclusions>
</dependency>

<!-- PrimeFaces FeedReader -->
<dependency>
<groupId>rome</groupId>
<artifactId>rome</artifactId>
<version>1.0</version>
</dependency>

<!-- PrimeFaces File Upload -->
<dependency>
<groupId>commons-fileupload</groupId>
<artifactId>commons-fileupload</artifactId>
<version>1.2.1</version>
</dependency>

<!-- PrimeFaces Themes (Individually)
<dependency>
<groupId>org.primefaces.themes</groupId>
<artifactId>cupertino</artifactId>
<version>1.0.8</version>
</dependency>
<dependency>
<groupId>org.primefaces.themes</groupId>
<artifactId>redmond</artifactId>
<version>1.0.8</version>
</dependency>
-->

<!-- PrimeFaces Themes (All) -->
<dependency>
<groupId>org.primefaces.themes</groupId>
<artifactId>all-themes</artifactId>
<version>1.0.9</version>
</dependency>

...
</project>
```

Now that we have completed the basic steps to create a PrimeFaces project, let's import the sample project for the book into Eclipse. It will give us a more full-featured example of what a PrimeFaces application looks like and we will study it in detail throughout this book. The following steps assume that you are running Windows or Mac OS X and will help you import the project:

1. Install the GitHub client (for Windows users, you can install the GitHub client at `http://windows.github.com`, and for Mac users please visit `http://mac.github.com`).

2. Navigate to `https://github.com/ianhlavats/primefaces-starter`.

3. Click the **Clone** button to copy the code to your computer.

4. In Eclipse, navigate to **File | Import | General | Existing Projects Into Workspace**.

5. Browse to the folder where you cloned the project.

6. Click on **OK** to import the **primefaces-webapp** project into the workspace.

The `pom.xml` file for the sample project contains everything you need to begin using PrimeFaces UI Components, PrimeFaces Themes, PrimeFaces Mobile, and PrimePush in your projects. We have also added Maven dependencies for **Contexts and Dependency Injection (CDI)**, Hibernate, MySQL, and have configured the Maven build process to use the Java SE 6 compiler and to generate Java Persistence API version 2 (JPA2) metamodel classes for type-safe criteria queries. There is a lot going on in this `pom.xml` file! Once you import the sample project, Maven will download the necessary JAR files and Eclipse will compile the code.

And that's it

We have created a new web application and installed PrimeFaces using Maven. We also imported the sample application for this book for reference. We will now look at developing, deploying, and running our application in the next section.

Downloading the example code

You can download the example code files for all Packt books you have purchased from your account at `http://www.packtpub.com`. If you purchased this book elsewhere, you can visit `http://www.packtpub.com/support` and register to have the files e-mailed directly to you.

Quick start – Implementing a sample project using PrimeFaces

In this section, we will get things started quickly by introducing the sample project that we will implement using PrimeFaces. This project will give us the opportunity to use the full spectrum of PrimeFaces Ajax components, the PrimeFaces Mobile Toolkit, and Prime Push technology.

Our client has a great idea for a web application: they want to build a website called *Show Time Guru* where people can meet and find fun and interesting things to do in their city.

Let's review the project requirements, architecture, and design before we implement our first JSF page using PrimeFaces.

Step 1 – Requirements

The client has provided us with the following requirements for the web application. Users will be able to do the following:

+ Sign up and log in to the application
+ Add, remove, and edit shows and events
+ Search for events using different criteria
+ See events in their city on a map
+ Rate shows and events they have attended
+ Connect with friends on the site
+ View charts on a dashboard showing event and site information
+ Access the application from a desktop computer or mobile device

Step 2 – Architecture and Design

The client presented us with a functional specification for the website. Our development team defined the application architecture, database schema, and site map diagram. Next we designed UI mockups and presented them to the client for approval.

Application Architecture

The following figure represents the application architecture:

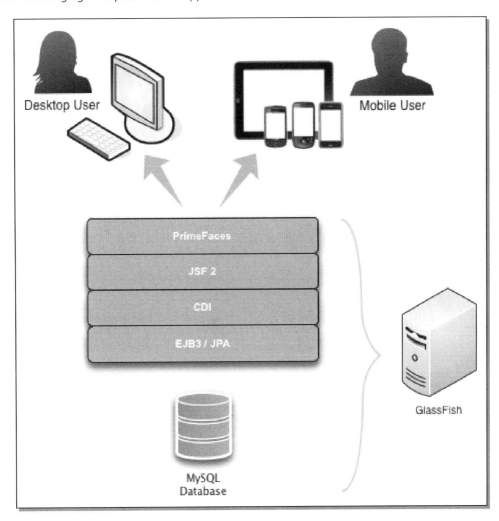

The Presentation tier will be implemented using JSF2 and PrimeFaces components. The Application tier will be based on Java EE 6 APIs and will use Contexts and Dependency Injection (CDI), EJB3, and JPA to communicate with the database. The Data tier will use a MySQL database. The application will be deployed as a WAR file to the GlassFish 3 application server.

Database Design

The following Entity Relationship (ER) diagram presents the Show Time Guru application's database schema:

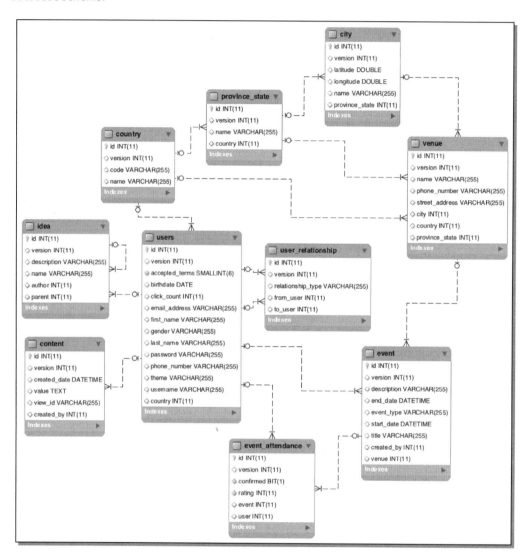

The database includes the following tables:

+ users: This stores user information
+ idea: This is a self-referential table for idea graphs
+ content: This stores web page CMS content
+ user_relationship: This represents a relationship between two users

- **country**: This stores names of countries, and is linked to users and venues
- **province_state**: This stores the names of provinces or states, and is linked to users and venues
- **venue**: This stores the location where an event is taking place
- **event**: This stores details of a movie, concert, or other social or entertainment event
- **event_attendance**: This records a user's attendance at an event

 Hibernate/JPA will create these tables automatically when you run the sample application. The persistence.xml file and the Java annotations in our domain model classes tell Hibernate which tables to create.

Information Architecture

The following site map diagram shows the different views and information architecture of the application, and how the site will look when organized on the file system:

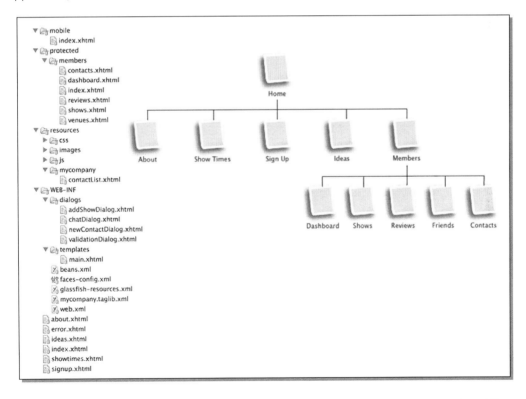

You can proceed by creating this folder structure in your primefaces-starter project. We will add the files throughout the rest of the book.

User Interface Design

We will be implementing these views using PrimeFaces components, so let's take a moment to understand the function of each page by looking at UI mockups. This will help us make the transition from the design to the implementation stage of the project, and will help us translate the client's vision for the site into a functional web application.

✦ The Home page will do the following:

      ◦ Provide information about the application

      ◦ Allow the user to log in

      ◦ Provide a link to a registration page

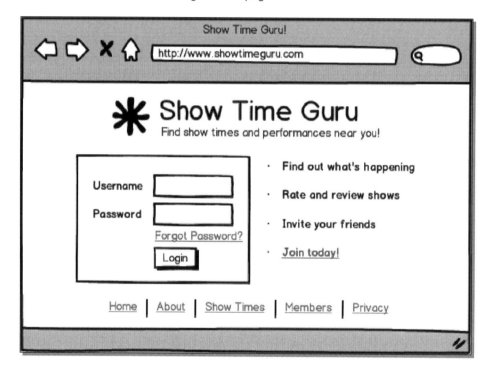

✦ The About page will do the following:

  ◦ Explain the motivation behind the site

  ◦ Contain text as shown in the UI mockup

  ◦ Provide a rich text editor for the user to edit the page content

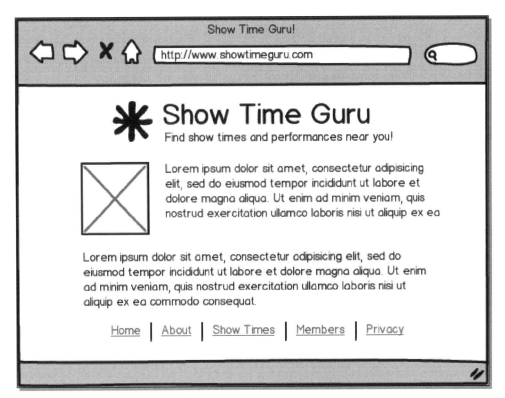

✦ The Show Times page is an important view in the application. It will do the following:

  ○ Provide a search screen for users to find events using different criteria, such as city, event type, and keywords

  ○ Show the results on a Google map

  ○ Show overlays with the event and venue information

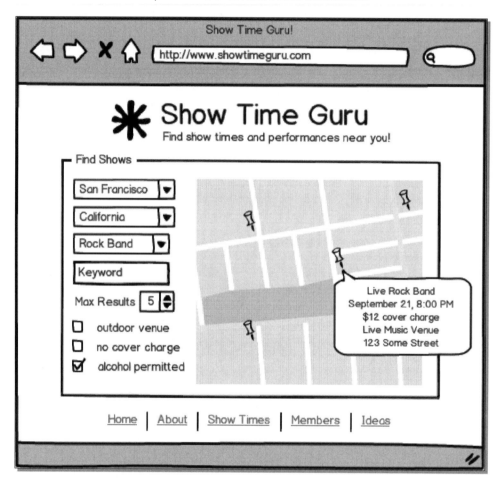

✦ The Sign up page will do the following:

- Display a registration form for new users to sign up
- Include the fields: **First name**, **Last name**, **Date of Birth**, **Country**, **City**, and more
- Include a CAPTCHA challenge to verify that the user is a person

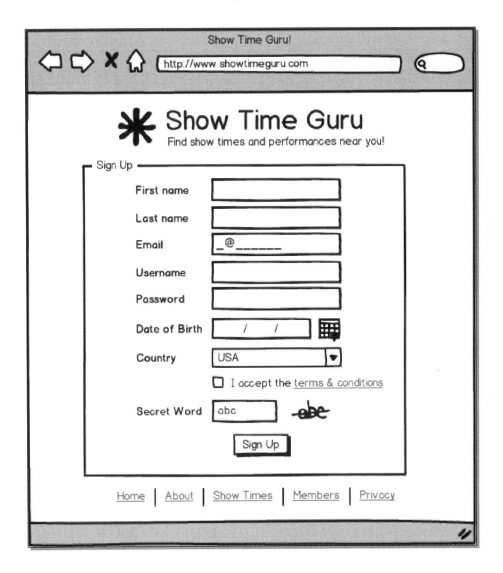

♦ Once the users log in, they will be directed to the Member page. This page contains a tabbed user interface that contains the following tabs:

　　º **Dashboard**: The **Dashboard** tab allows the user to view data about events in various chart formats.

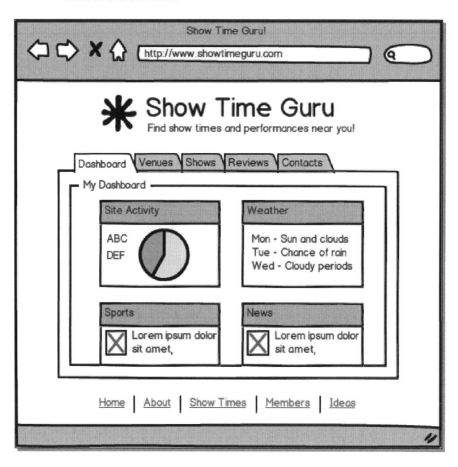

○ **Venues**: The **Venues** tab displays a form for entering new venues and editing existing ones.

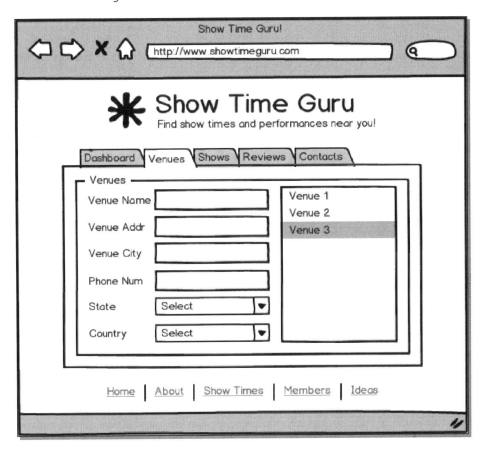

○ **Shows**: The **Shows** tab displays a calendar of shows the user has submitted. It also enables the user to add new shows and delete existing ones.

○ **Reviews**: The **Reviews** tab provides a view of past events, and enables the user to comment on and rate these events.

○ **Contacts**: The **Contacts** tab provides an address book interface for the user to manage his or her friend list. The user can connect with friends, family, and colleagues, and have a live chat with contacts that are also on the site.

✦ The Ideas page is a creative space where users can brainstorm about new events. They can create a mind map diagram to store ideas for future events.

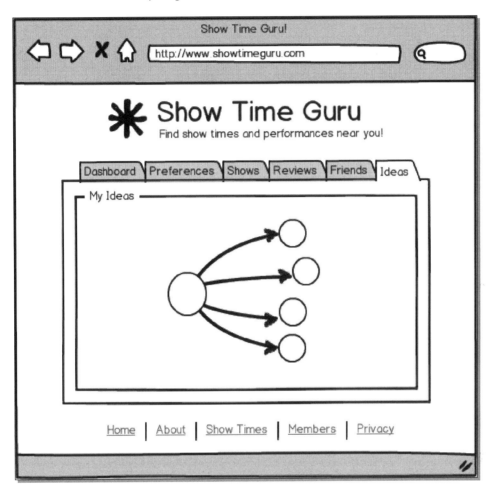

Step 3 – Implementation

In this section, we will implement the Home page of the application. The instructions assume that you are using Dreamweaver as your web authoring tool to create and edit JSF pages, but you can use Eclipse or your editor of choice. We will use Eclipse for developing, compiling, packaging, and deploying Java code.

Step 1 – Creating the Directory Structure

The first step is to create the directory structure for the web application in the `src/main/webapp` folder of the primefaces-starter project we set up in the *Installation* section. You can follow the example from the `primefaces-webapp` project as a reference, or refer back to the site map diagram in the *Information Architecture* section for guidelines.

The `resources` folder is for our JSF2 resource libraries. The `WEB-INF/templates` folder contains our Facelets template. The `beans.xml` file enables CDI support for our webapp. The `faces-config.xml` file is required by JSF to enable JSF2 functionality. The `glassfish-resources.xml` file defines the MySQL data source and connection pool that will be deployed to GlassFish for our application. The `web.xml` file is the standard Java web application deployment descriptor.

Step 2 – Creating the Facelets Template

Facelets provides an advanced templating system we can leverage to simplify our page layouts and user interface development. Facelets templating involves a UI template that defines the template regions (for example, head content, page header, body content, footer, and so on), and one or more pages (also called **template clients**) that use the UI template and fill in its regions with view-specific information.

Let's create a Facelets UI template that provides a common header and footer for our pages while defining view-specific title and content regions that will be implemented by each page. Open your web page authoring tool and create a new file named `main.xhtml` in the `src/main/webapp/WEB-INF/templates` folder with the following code:

```
<!DOCTYPE html PUBLIC "-//W3C//DTD XHTML 1.0 Transitional//EN"
"http://www.w3.org/TR/xhtml1/DTD/xhtml1-transitional.dtd">
<html xmlns="http://www.w3.org/1999/xhtml"
      xmlns:h="http://java.sun.com/jsf/html"
      xmlns:ui="http://java.sun.com/jsf/facelets"
      xmlns:p="http://primefaces.org/ui">
<h:head>
<meta http-equiv="Content-Type" content="text/html; charset=utf-8" />
<title><ui:insert name="title" /></title>
<h:outputStylesheet library="css" name="main.css" />
</h:head>
<body>
<div class="header">
<h:graphicImage library="images" name="showtime_logo.png" />
</div>
<div class="content">
<ui:insert name="content" />
</div>
```

```
<div class="footer">
<!-- Footer links here are omitted -->
</div>
</body>
</html>
```

Our Facelets UI template is very simple, and includes only a title region and content region. Each page that uses this template will inherit the HTML and will be able to provide its own page title and user interface content.

Step 3 – Creating the Login Page

The login page is named `index.xhtml` and contains the following code:

```
<!DOCTYPE html PUBLIC "-//W3C//DTD XHTML 1.0 Transitional//EN"
"http://www.w3.org/TR/xhtml1/DTD/xhtml1-transitional.dtd">
<html xmlns="http://www.w3.org/1999/xhtml"
      xmlns:ui="http://java.sun.com/jsf/facelets"
      xmlns:h="http://java.sun.com/jsf/html"
      xmlns:p="http://primefaces.org/ui">
<h:head />
<body>
<ui:composition template="/WEB-INF/templates/main.xhtml">
<ui:define name="title">Welcome to our site</ui:define>
<ui:define name="content">
<h:form>
<h:panelGrid columns="2" border="0">
<p:panel header="Please Sign In">
<p:panelGrid columns="2" styleClass="no-border"
columnClasses="no-border,no-border">
<p:outputLabel value="Username" for="username" />
<p:inputText id="username" label="Username"
             value="#{credentials.username}" />
<p:outputLabel value="Password" for="password" />
<p:password id="password" label="Password"
             value="#{credentials.password}" />
<h:outputText value="" />
<p:commandLink value="Forgot your password?" />
<h:outputText value="" />
<p:commandButton value="Login" action="members"
actionListener="#{loginController.login}" />
<h:outputText value="" />
</p:panelGrid>
</p:panel>
<ul>
```

```
<li>Find out what's happening</li>
<li>Rate and review shows</li>
<li>Invite your friends</li>
<li><a href="/faces/register.xhtml">Join
today!</a></li>
</ul>
</h:panelGrid>
</h:form>
</ui:define>
</ui:composition>
</body>
</html>
```

Step 4 – Implementing the LoginController Class

Our application is based on the **Model-View-Controller** (**MVC**) architecture. The Model is composed of JPA-enabled domain model classes that represent the nouns in our application, such as `User`, `Event`, and `EventAttendance`. These model classes are persistent, meaning their state is saved in our database. We use Hibernate's JPA implementation for **Object-Relational Mapping** (**ORM**) between our domain model and the database.

The login screen represents a typical View in our application. These views are implemented as Facelets XHTML pages and use the **Expression Language** (**EL**) to bind user interface components to controller event handlers and model attributes. In the preceding example, two text fields are bound to the `username` and `password` attributes of the `Credentials` model object using the EL expressions `#{credentials.username}` and `#{credentials.password}`. These are called value expressions because they display and update a value by calling getter and setter methods of the model object. The expression `#{loginController.login}` is called a method expression because it invokes application logic in the controller.

The `LoginController` class, as the name suggests, is a Controller designed to handle user interface events from the login screen. It is implemented as a view-scoped JSF managed bean, meaning the object is created by JSF and its lifecycle is scoped to the current view. Once the user navigates to another view, the `LoginController` object is released and will eventually be garbage-collected by the JVM. The following UML class diagram describes this class and shows how it relates to other JSF controllers, CDI-managed services, and JPA domain model classes:

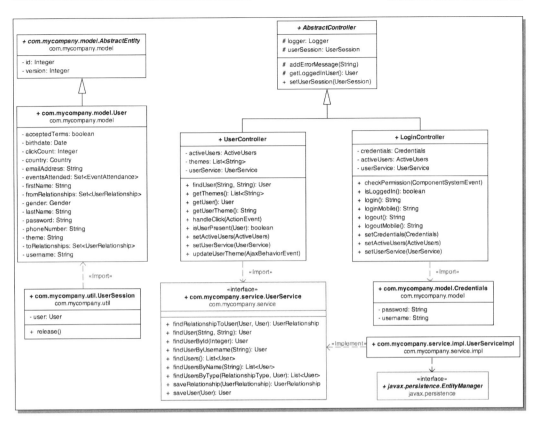

The `LoginController` class is responsible for authenticating the user represented by the `User` class. The user's credentials are stored in a `Credentials` object and the user interface invokes the `login()` method of the `LoginController` class to authenticate. This method delegates to the CDI-managed `UserServiceImpl` stateless session bean class to look up the user in the database. If the user is found, this method stores the `User` object in a session-scoped bean named `userSession` and adds the user to an application-scoped `List` object named `activeUsers` for presence purposes. The `release()` method of the `UserSession` class removes the user from the `activeUsers` list when the session expires.

Note that, although we annotated the fields with the JSF `@ManagedProperty` annotation, JSF uses setter injection, so we must also declare setters for these dependencies. Both `LoginController` and `UserController` are subclasses of `AbstractController`, a superclass that provides a logger object and JSF API convenience methods.

```
@ManagedBean
@ViewScoped
public class LoginController extends AbstractController {
```

```java
@ManagedProperty(value = "#{activeUsers}")
private ActiveUsers activeUsers;

@ManagedProperty(value = "#{credentials}")
private Credentials credentials;

@ManagedProperty(value = "#{userService}")
private UserService userService;

public String login() {
    String outcome = null;
    try {
        String username = credentials.getUsername();
        String password = credentials.getPassword();
        User user = userService.findUser(username, password);
        if (user == null) {
            addErrorMessage("Invalid login");
            userSession.setUser(null);
        } else {
            userSession.setUser(user);
            if (!activeUsers.contains(user)) {
                activeUsers.add(user);
            }
            outcome = "members";
        }
    } catch (Exception e) {
        logger.error("Unable to login:", e);
    }
    return outcome;
}

//...
```

After successful authentication, the `login()` method returns the string `"members"` and JSF redirects the user to the member home page as per the navigation rule in our `faces-config.xml` file.

```xml
<navigation-rule>
<from-view-id>*</from-view-id>
<navigation-case>
<from-outcome>members</from-outcome>
<to-view-id>/protected/members/index.xhtml</to-view-id>
<redirect />
</navigation-case>
</navigation-rule>
```

The `UserServiceImpl` class is annotated with the `@Named` annotation, exposing it to the JSF layer for dependency injection, and with the `@Stateless` annotation, giving it transaction support for accessing the database. `UserServiceImpl` uses the JPA Entity Manager API to look up the user in the database.

```
@Named("userService")
@Stateless
public class UserServiceImpl extends AbstractService implements
    UserService {

    @Override
    public User findUser(String username, String password) {
        TypedQuery<User> query =
        em.createNamedQuery(Queries.USER_FIND_BY_USERNAME_PASSWORD,
        User.class);
        query.setParameter(1, username);
        query.setParameter(2, password);
        List<User> users = query.getResultList();
        if (!users.isEmpty()) {
            return users.get(0);
        }
        return null;
    }

}
```

`UserServiceImpl` executes a JPA-named query defined in the `User` class; and, if the user is found, `LoginController` will store the user in the `UserSession` JSF-managed bean for the duration of the user's session.

```
@Entity
// ...
@NamedQueries({ @NamedQuery(name = Queries.USER_FIND_BY_USERNAME_
PASSWORD, query = "select u from User u where u.username=?1 and
u.password=?2"), ... })
public class User extends AbstractEntity {
// ...
}
```

To see the full source code for this example, please refer to the `primefaces-webapp` sample project. Take some time to study the code, and use it as a guideline for implementing the login screen in your `primefaces-starter` project. Feel free to copy the sample code into your project as a starting point for your own code, or to start from a clean slate for your own implementation. If you like, you can simply run the sample code for now to become familiar with all the moving parts of a PrimeFaces application, and implement your own solution once you have studied the code.

Step 5 – Deploying the web application

We are ready to test our web application in the browser. To deploy the project to GlassFish using Eclipse, select the **Servers** tab then right-click on **GlassFish** and choose **Add and Remove**. Select the **primefaces-webapp** project on the left-hand side and click on the **Add** button to configure it for deployment. Click on **Finish** and Eclipse will publish the project to GlassFish. Once you have the sample application up and running, feel free to deploy your own project in the same way.

Step 6 – Opening the web application in the browser

Open your web browser and navigate to `http://localhost:8080/primefaces-webapp/faces/index.xhtml`.

You should see a login screen, as shown in the the following screenshot:

There it is! We have developed the first screen in our client's web application. In the next section, we will implement additional views for both the desktop and mobile user interfaces of our application.

Top 3 features you need to know about

In the last section, we outlined an application architecture and user interface design for a PrimeFaces web application. In this section, we will look at how to implement additional views in the application for desktop and mobile users and will use the sample project as a showcase for the following top 3 features:

* **PrimeFaces**: An Ajax-enabled UI component toolkit for developing JSF applications for desktop web browsers
* **PrimeFaces Mobile**: A set of UI components based on jQuery Mobile for developing JSF applications for mobile web browsers
* **PrimePush**: An Ajax Push framework that supports Comet, WebSockets and other protocols for asynchronous server-to-browser communication. We will discuss these features in detail as we implement the screens for the application.

User sign-up page

Since our signup page will be one of the first screens that most users see, let's start by implementing this view.

Sign-up controller implementation

First, we need a JSF-managed bean to act as a controller for user interface events on our sign-up page. The `SignUpController` class will implement this functionality. Once again we will use a view-scoped JSF managed bean with dependencies on CDI-managed stateless services and references to JPA domain model classes.

```
@ManagedBean
@ViewScoped
public class SignupController extends AbstractController {

    @ManagedProperty(value = "#{countryService}")
    private CountryService countryService;

    private User user;

    @ManagedProperty(value = "#{userService}")
    private UserService userService;

    // ...

    public String signup() {
        if (isValidUser()) {
            userService.saveUser(user);
            return "login";
        }
        return null;
    }

}
```

The following UML diagram describes how `SignUpController` is associated with other CDI and JPA classes in our application. JSF classes have Controller in the class name and are located in the `com.mycompany.controller` package, while CDI classes are in the `com.mycompany. service` package, and JPA classes are in the `com.mycompany.model` package.

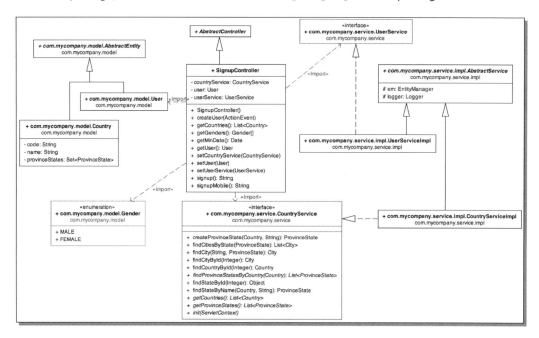

`SignUpController` is composed of a `User` object from our JPA domain model. In MVC and object-oriented terminology, this controller *has-a* model. This controller also has references to the `Country` and `Gender` model classes for populating fields in the signup form. The `signup()` method is responsible for validating the uniqueness of the username in our database and then saving the user. If successful, we return the "index" outcome to navigate to the login screen, otherwise we return `null` to stay on the same page so a message can be displayed and the user can correct any errors. Note that the controller does not have a direct dependency on the service implementation class, but only an indirect one through the service's interface. Also note that the service classes share a common superclass, as do the model and controller classes.

Sign-up page creation

Our sign-up page is located at `/signup.xhtml` and is based on the same Facelets template as our login page. For simplicity, we are only showing the relevant contents of this page in the following code snippet:

```
<h:form id="signupForm" styleClass="input-form">
...
<p:panel header="Sign Up" id="panel">
```

```
<p:messages id="messages" showDetail="true" showSummary="false"
            autoUpdate="true"/>
<h:panelGrid columns="2">
<p:outputLabel value="First Name" for="firstname" />
<p:inputText id="firstname" label="First Name"
             value="#{signupController.user.firstName}"
             required="true" />
<p:outputLabel value="Last Name" for="lastname" />
...
<p:outputLabel value="Phone Number" for="phone" />
<p:inputMask id="phone" label="Phone Number"
             value="#{signupController.user.phoneNumber}"
             required="true" mask="(999) 999-9999" />
...
<p:outputLabel value="Password" for="password" />
<p:password id="password" label="Password"
            value="#{signupController.user.password}"
            feedback="true" required="true" match="password2" />
<p:outputLabel value="Confirm" for="password2" />
<p:password id="password2" label="Password"
            value="#{signupController.user.password}"
            feedback="false" required="true" />
<p:outputLabel value="Gender" for="gender" />
<p:selectOneRadio id="gender" style="float:left" required="true"
                  value="#{signupController.user.gender}">
<f:selectItems value="#{signupController.genders}"
               itemLabel="#{gender.label}"
               itemValue="#{gender}" var="gender" />
</p:selectOneRadio>
<p:outputLabel value="Date of birth" for="birthdate" />
<p:calendar id="birthdate" value="#{signupController.user.
birthdate}"navigator="true" required="true" yearRange="c-100:c-0"
pattern="MM/dd/yyyy" showOn="button" readonlyInput="true"/>
<p:outputLabel value="Country" for="country" />
<p:selectOneMenu value="#{signupController.user.country}"
                 id="country" required="true">
<f:selectItems value="#{countryController.countries}"
               var="country" itemValue="#{country}"
               itemLabel="#{country.name}" />
</p:selectOneMenu>
<h:outputText value="" />
<h:panelGroup>
<p:selectBooleanCheckbox required="true" id="terms"
    label="Accept terms and conditions"
value="#{signupController.user.acceptedTerms}"
widgetVar="termsCheckbox" />
<p:outputLabel value="I accept the terms and conditions"
               onclick="termsCheckbox.toggle()" for="terms" />
</h:panelGroup>
```

```
<p:outputLabel for="captcha" value="Secret Word" />
<p:captcha required="true" id="captcha" />
</h:panelGrid>
<p:commandButton value="Sign Up"
                 action="#{signupController.signup}"
                 style="display:block; margin:0 auto;"
                 ajax="false" />
</p:panel>
...
</h:form>
```

This following screenshot shows the user signup page for our webapp in the browser. The PrimeFaces password strength indicator and CAPTCHA components add nice security features to our application:

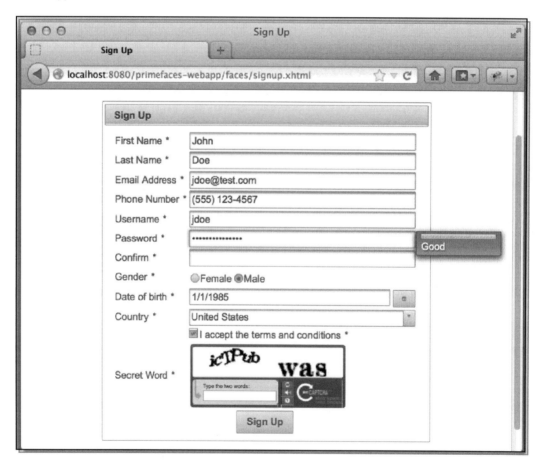

This example demonstrates how to use a number of common PrimeFaces input components. First, we use the PrimeFaces panel container with a header for the form fields. Inside the panel we have the standard JSF panelGrid with two columns for label and field.

We are using the PrimeFaces `label` component for all labels, as it has additional capabilities such as rendering an asterisk automatically for required fields and highlighting itself in red when a required field is empty. The label's `for` attribute references the input component ID attribute. These attributes are critical for this enhanced functionality, so don't make the mistake of forgetting to specify them.

The **First Name**, **Last Name**, **Email Address**, and **Username** fields are using the PrimeFaces `inputText` component. This component also highlights itself in red when user input is missing or invalid. JSF Core validator tags such as `validateLength` can be used with this component in the same way they are used with standard JSF HTML `inputText` component.

The **Phone Number** field is using the PrimeFaces `inputMask` component to provide the `(999) 999-9999` mask for user input. Any non-numeric input or value that does not match the pattern will be ignored by this component.

Phone Number * (555) 123-____

The **Password** and **Confirm Password** fields are both implemented using the PrimeFaces `password` component. The first password component has the `feedback="true"` and `match="password2"` attributes, while the second password component does not. These attributes tell PrimeFaces to display a password strength feedback indicator while the user is typing in the first field, and to compare the two passwords to make sure they are the same.

The `password` component is a good example of how PrimeFaces UI components have a high level of built-in usability that can be enabled with minimal effort. We will see this same quality in many other PrimeFaces components.

The **Gender** field is implemented using the PrimeFaces `selectOneRadio` component. This component uses a Java enum for its values. The EL expression `#{signupController.genders}` simply returns an array of `Gender` enum objects:

```
public Gender[] getGenders() {
    return Gender.values();
}
```

The **Date of Birth** field uses the PrimeFaces `calendar` component. The `navigator="true"` attribute renders the year as a drop-down menu, the `showOn="button"` attribute renders a toggle button that shows and hides the pop-up calendar, and the `yearRange="c-100:c-0"` attribute renders a list of years going back 100 years from the current date.

The **Country** field uses the PrimeFaces `selectOneMenu` component to render a list of `Country` objects from our database, and JSF calls our `CountryConverter` to handle object-to-string conversion:

```
@FacesConverter(forClass = Country.class)
public class CountryConverter implements Converter {
```

```
    @Override
    public Object getAsObject(FacesContext context, UIComponent
        component, String value) {
        if (value == null) {
            return null;
        }
        CountryService service = (CountryService)
        FacesUtils.getManagedBean("countryService");
        return service.findCountryById(Integer.valueOf(value));
    }

    @Override
    public String getAsString(FacesContext context, UIComponent
        component, Object value) {
        if (value instanceof Country) {
            return String.valueOf(((Country) value).getId());
        } else if (value instanceof String) {
            return ((String) value);
        }
        return null;
    }
}
```

We use the JSF `@FacesConverter` annotation to avoid XML configuration, and as the `Country` class is part of our JPA domain model, it has a unique primary key ID that can be used for conversion. This converter simply delegates to the `CountryService` class to call `findCountryById(Integer)` to look up the country in our database.

`FacesUtils` is a utility class that provides a method for looking up a JSF-managed bean:

```
    public static Object getManagedBean(String name) {
        FacesContext ctx = FacesContext.getCurrentInstance();
        return ctx.getApplication().evaluateExpressionGet(ctx,
        "#{" + name + "}", Object.class);
    }
```

We use the CDI events feature to call `CountryService.init()` when the application is started, so it can populate our database with country data (see the Java EE 6 tutorial for more information on CDI events, at `http://docs.oracle.com/javaee/6/tutorial/doc/gkhic.html`).

```
    @Override
    public void init(@Observes @Initialized ServletContext context) throws
        Exception {
        List<Country> countries = getCountries();
        if (countries == null || countries.isEmpty()) {
            logger.info("Importing country and city data...");
            importCountries();
            importCities();
        }
    }
```

Next, we use the PrimeFaces `selectBooleanCheckbox` component to render the "accept terms and conditions" field, and finally we use the PrimeFaces `CAPTCHA` component to render a `reCAPTCHA` widget to ensure only real people are signing up.

 The PrimeFaces `CAPTCHA` component requires a valid public and private key to be registered in the application's `web.xml` file. You can sign up for a free account on `http://recaptcha.net` to get your keys.

The PrimeFaces `commandButton` component at the bottom of the screen has the `ajax="false"` attribute to submit the form without Ajax for best compatibility with the `CAPTCHA` component. If the user is registered successfully after clicking the **Sign Up** button, we navigate to the login screen. If you want to use Ajax to submit the form, you will need to add `oncomplete="Recaptcha.reload()"` to the command button to reload the CAPTCHA component after the Ajax request.

Dashboard page

This Dashboard page demonstrates a number of key features of the PrimeFaces UI component library:

It includes the following features:

✦ PrimeFaces themes

+ Enabling drag-and-drop support
+ Using Ajax effects
+ Dynamic charts
+ Working with panels
+ Modal status indicator
+ Using RSS feeds in your PrimeFaces application

To handle events and provide a model for our dashboard, we implement a
`DashboardController` class as a JSF-managed bean. This class produces a dashboard
model named `DashboardModel` that stores the number of columns and the panels in
each column. The dashboard model is initialized in the constructor of the class as follows:

```
public DashboardController() {
    model = new DefaultDashboardModel();
    DashboardColumn column1 = new DefaultDashboardColumn();
    DashboardColumn column2 = new DefaultDashboardColumn();
    DashboardColumn column3 = new DefaultDashboardColumn();
    column1.addWidget("sports");
    column1.addWidget("events");
    column2.addWidget("weather");
    column2.addWidget("clicks");
    column3.addWidget("politics");
    column3.addWidget("entertainment");
    model.addColumn(column1);
    model.addColumn(column2);
    model.addColumn(column3);
}
```

Next, we use the PrimeFaces dashboard component in our JSF page, bind it to `DashboardModel`,
and declare an Ajax event handler for reorder events fired when the user drags and drops a
dashboard panel.

```
<p:dashboard model="#{dashboardController.model}"
             id="dashboard">
<p:ajax event="reorder"
        listener="#{dashboardController.handleReorder}" />
```

We include a number of `panel` components to define our dashboard widgets. The
`DashboardModel` will determine which widgets are visible, and in which column,
based on a match between the ID of the `panel` component and the string passed to
`DashboardColumn.addWidget()`.

```
<p:panel id="events" header="Event Turnout" toggleable="true"
  closable="true" toggleSpeed="500" closeSpeed="500"
```

```
    widgetVar="eventsPanelWidget">
<!-- Content -->
</p:panel>
```

Notice that we can define attributes of the dashboard panel, namely, the header, toggle ability and speed, close ability, and so on. The `widgetVar` attribute is important because it allows us to interact with the PrimeFaces component using the component's JavaScript API.

 The PrimeFaces JavaScript API exposes a lot of functionality for client-side user interaction with PrimeFaces UI components. Please see the PrimeFaces User Guide available from `http://www.primefaces.org` for details.

In the following example, we define custom actions for the dashboard widget using the `actions` facet of the `panel` component:

```
<p:panel id="entertainment" header="Entertainment"
        toggleable="true" closable="true" toggleSpeed="500"
        closeSpeed="500" widgetVar="entertainmentPanelWidget">
<f:facet name="actions">
<p:commandLink styleClass="ui-panel-titlebar-icon ui-corner-all ui-
state-default">
<h:outputText styleClass="ui-icon ui-icon-star" />
<p:effect type="explode" event="click" for="entertainment" />
</p:commandLink>
</f:facet>
<!-- Content -->
</p:panel>
```

Our dashboard page includes the PrimeFaces `themeSwitcher` component to enable the user to change the theme dynamically. It updates the look and feel of the whole user interface without a full page refresh!

```
<p:themeSwitcher value="#{userController.user.theme}"
                style="width:165px" effect="fade"
                id="statefulSwitcher">
<f:selectItem itemLabel="Select a Theme" itemValue="#{null}" />
<f:selectItems value="#{userController.themes}" />
<p:ajax listener="#{userController.updateUserTheme}" />
</p:themeSwitcher>
```

Dashboard widgets can also include PrimeFaces charting components. Our `Event Turnout` widget shows the overall attendance for recent events in the calendar. This panel uses the PrimeFaces `barChart` component bound to a `CartesianChartModel` in our backing bean:

```
<p:panel id="events" header="Event Turnout"
         toggleable="true" closable="true"
         toggleSpeed="500" closeSpeed="500"
         widgetVar="eventsPanelWidget">
    <p:barChart id="basic"
                value="#{chartController.barChartModel}"
                rendered="#{chartController.barChartModel ne null}"
                legendPosition="ne" min="0" max="10"
                style="height:200px"/>
</p:panel>
```

The bar chart model uses a JPA query to get demographic data about the people who attended recent events as an array of objects. The `ChartService` class executes the following JPA named query to get the data.

```
select e.event.startDate, count(e.user.gender) from EventAttendance
e where e.user.gender = ?1 and e.confirmed is true group by e.event
order by e.event.startDate
```

The preceding query returns a list of `Object` arrays representing the number of males or females who attended each event. The first element in each array is the event date, and the second element is the number of male or female users who attended:

```
private void createBarChartModel() {
    List<Object[]> maleResults =
    chartService.findEventAttendanceByGender(Gender.MALE);
    List<Object[]> femaleResults =
    chartService.findEventAttendanceByGender(Gender.FEMALE);
    if (maleResults.isEmpty() && femaleResults.isEmpty()) {
        return;
    }
    barChartModel = new CartesianChartModel();
    ChartSeries males = buildChartSeries(maleResults, "Male");
    ChartSeries females = buildChartSeries(femaleResults, "Female");
    barChartModel.addSeries(males);
    barChartModel.addSeries(females);
}
```

Next we pass this array to a method to build a PrimeFaces `ChartSeries` object from the data.

```
private ChartSeries buildChartSeries(List<Object[]> results, String
    label) {
    ChartSeries series = new ChartSeries();
    series.setLabel(label);
    // calculate monthly totals
```

```
        SimpleDateFormat sdf = new SimpleDateFormat("MMM/yy");
        List<String> months = new ArrayList<String>();
        Map<String, Long> monthTotals = new HashMap<String, Long>();
        for (Object[] result : results) {
            Date date = (Date) result[0];
            Long count = (Long) result[1];
            String month = sdf.format(date);
            if (!months.contains(month)) {
                months.add(month);
            }
            Long total = monthTotals.get(month);
            if (total == null) {
                total = 0L;
            }
            monthTotals.put(month, count + total);
        }
        // add the data to the chart series
        for (String month : months) {
            series.set(month, monthTotals.get(month).intValue());
        }
        return series;
    }
```

We add two ChartSeries objects to the BarChartModel and bind it to the barChart component's value attribute to render the data. See how easy it is to use PrimeFaces charting components?

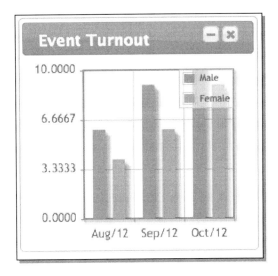

The following is a UML diagram that describes how we implemented `ChartController`:

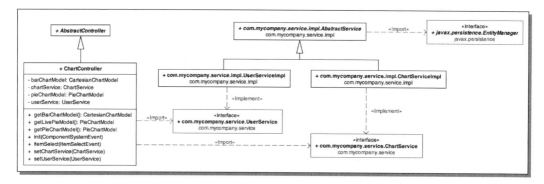

`ChartController` is a `@ViewScoped` JSF-managed bean that extends `AbstractController` and depends on the CDI managed `UserService` and `ChartService` stateless services to fetch data for the PrimeFaces charting components.

Similarly, our `Clicks` dashboard widget uses the PrimeFaces `pieChart` component to render a pie chart showing how many times users clicked the link above the chart.

```
<p:panel id="clicks" header="Clicks" toggleable="true"
         closable="true" toggleSpeed="500"
         closeSpeed="500" widgetVar="clicksPanelWidget"
         style="text-align:center">
<p:commandLink id="clickLink" value="Click"
               actionListener="#{userController.handleClick}"
               update="clicks" />
<p:pieChart id="votes"
            value="#{chartController.pieChartModel}"
            style="height:185px" legendPosition="nw"
            legendRows="6" legendCols="1"
            showDataLabels="true" dataFormat="value" />
</p:panel>
```

`UserController` updates the current user's click count in the database and replaces the `User` object in the session with the updated object:

```
public void handleClick(ActionEvent event) {
    User user = getUser();
    if (user != null) {
        Integer count = user.getClickCount();
        if (count == null) {
            count = 0;
        }
        user.setClickCount(count + 1);
        user = userService.saveUser(user);
```

```
        userSession.setUser(user);
    }
}
```

Next, we create a `PieChartModel` containing the click count for all users as its data source. In this case, we fetch all `User` objects from the database and iterate the collection. For each user, we create a pie chart section for the user with the click count as the value.

```
private void createPieModel() {
    pieChartModel = new PieChartModel();
    List<User> users = userService.findUsers();
    for (User user : users) {
        Integer count = user.getClickCount();
        if (count == null) {
            count = 0;
        }
        String username = user.getUsername();
        pieChartModel.getData().put(username, count);
    }
}
```

The result is a simple but effective pie chart showing clicks per user:

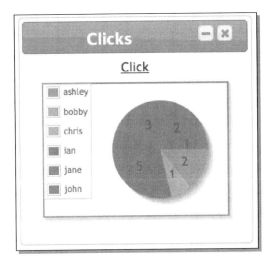

The remaining dashboard widgets demonstrate the use of the PrimeFaces `feedReader` component to transform a Yahoo! RSS feed into HTML at request time to display the latest news, sports, and entertainment info.

```
<p:panel id="sports" header="Sports" toggleable="true"
        closable="true" toggleSpeed="500" closeSpeed="500"
        widgetVar="sportsPanelWidget">
<p:feedReader value="http://rss.news.yahoo.com/rss/sports"
```

```
                        var="feed" size="1">
    <h:outputText value="#{feed.title}"
                    style="font-weight: bold; display:block"/>
    <h:outputText value="#{feed.description.value}" escape="false"/>
    </p:feedReader>
    </p:panel>
```

Venues page

In the following screenshot we can see a number of enhanced input components included with PrimeFaces, such as text fields, list boxes, tabs, buttons, and editable combo boxes. The screen shows a JSF information message after a successful save action using the enhanced PrimeFaces messages component.

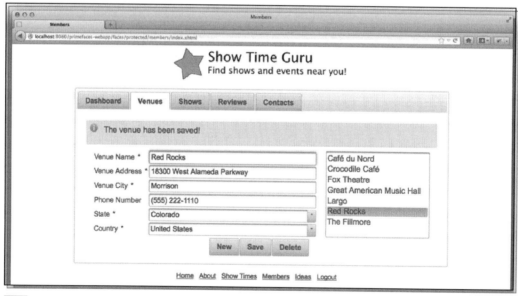

The **Venues** tab provides an interface for users of the website to add new venues for past and upcoming events. This tab also demonstrates some interesting UI controls provided by PrimeFaces.

Venue selection for editing

On this screen, the user can select an existing venue to edit. We use the PrimeFaces selectOneListbox component to display the names of the existing venues in the database. When the user selects a venue in the list, we use the PrimeFaces <p:ajax> tag to load the venue data for editing and re-render the form.

```
<p:selectOneListbox id="selectedVenue"
value="#{venueController.venue}"
style="width:275px; height:220px;"
valueChangeListener="#{venueController.venueSelected}">
<f:selectItems value="#{venueController.venues}" var="venue"
                itemLabel="#{venue.name}" itemValue="#{venue}" />
<p:ajax process="@this"
  update="venuePanel deleteButton confirmDialog" />
</p:selectOneListbox>
```

<p:ajax> versus <f:ajax>

The PrimeFaces <p:ajax> tag is similar to the standard JSF2 <f:ajax> tag, however the <p:ajax> tag has additional functionality and the <f:ajax> tag is not guaranteed to work with PrimeFaces components. The <p:ajax> tag also has additional support for PrimeFaces Mobile. In general, you should only use <p:ajax> with PrimeFaces.

Enhanced confirmation dialog

To enhance our venue configuration screen further, let's add an enhanced confirmation dialog component for smoother interaction with the user. This image displays the PrimeFaces confirmation dialog component. It has skinning capabilities, is easy to customize, and is not affected by pop-up blockers, so it provides a nice alternative to the built-in JavaScript `confirm()` dialog.

The PrimeFaces `confirmDialog` component has three important attributes for a basic confirmation dialog: `message`, `header`, and `widgetVar`. The message attribute defines the confirmation message, the header attribute defines the dialog header, and the widgetVar attribute names a JavaScript variable used to show and hide the confirm dialog.

```
<p:confirmDialog id="confirmDialog"
message="Are you sure you want to delete '#{venueController.venue.
name}'?&lt;br&gt;All related events will also be deleted."
header="Delete Venue" severity="alert"
widgetVar="confirmationWidget">
<div style="text-align:center">
<p:commandButton id="confirm" value="OK" update="venueForm"
                 oncomplete="confirmationWidget.hide()"
                 actionListener="#{venueController.deleteVenue}"
/>
<p:commandButton id="decline" value="Cancel"
                 onclick="confirmationWidget.hide()" type="button"
/>
</div>
</p:confirmDialog>
```

An editable select-one menu component

An interesting use case in UI development is supporting an editable list of values. Sometimes users want to be able to add items to a list of values that can then be selected later, for instance, a list of outcomes for a phone call or meeting. In our **Venues** tab, we can use this functionality to allow the user to populate the list of states, to demonstrate this technique.

This screenshot shows the user typing the value `Maine` into the state select field. The next time the user wants to add a venue for this state, he can simply select it from the list. This feature is implemented using the PrimeFaces `selectOneMenu` component and a custom JSF converter tag:

```
<html xmlns:mycompany="http://www.showtimeguru.com/taglib" ... >
...
<p:selectOneMenu value="#{venueController.venue.provinceState}"
id="venueState" style="width:453px"
required="true" editable="true"
disabled="#{venueController.venue.country eq null}">
<f:param id="countryParam"
        value="#{venueController.venue.country}" />
<f:selectItem itemLabel="Select" itemValue="#{null}" />
<f:selectItems value="#{countryController.findProvinceStatesByCountry(
venueController.venue.country)}"
            var="state" itemLabel="#{state.name}"
            itemValue="#{state}" />
<mycompany:editableStateConverter />
</p:selectOneMenu>
```

To support the editing function, we implemented a special JSF converter that can save a new province or state to the database.

```
@FacesConverter(forClass = ProvinceState.class, value = "mycompany.
EditableStateConverter")
```

```
public class EditableStateConverter implements Converter {

    @Override
    public Object getAsObject(FacesContext context, UIComponent
    component, String value) {
        if (value == null) {
            return null;
        }
        ProvinceState state = null;
        UIParameter param = (UIParameter) component.
        findComponent("countryParam");
        if (param != null) {
            // lookup existing state by country and name
            Country country = (Country) param.getValue();
            CountryService service = (CountryService)
            FacesUtils.getManagedBean("countryService");
            state = service.findStateByName(country, value);
            if (state == null) {
                // create new state if it does not exist
                state = service.createProvinceState(country, value);
            }
        }
        return state;
    }

    // ...

}
```

We also create a Facelets custom tag library file name `mycompany.taglib.xml` and add this to our WEB-INF folder. We declare a custom tag named `<mycompany:editableStateConverter>` that simply delegates to our converter:

```
<?xml version="1.0" encoding="UTF-8"?>
<facelet-taglib xmlns="http://java.sun.com/xml/ns/javaee"
   xmlns:xsi="http://www.w3.org/2001/XMLSchema-instance"
   xsi:schemaLocation="http://java.sun.com/xml/ns/javaee http://java.
sun.com/xml/ns/javaee/web-facelettaglibrary_2_0.xsd"
   version="2.0">
<description>My Company Custom Facelets Tag Library</description>
<display-name>My Company Tag Library</display-name>
<namespace>http://www.showtimeguru.com/taglib</namespace>
<tag>
<tag-name>editableStateConverter</tag-name>
<converter>
<converter-id>mycompany.EditableStateConverter</converter
-id>
</converter>
</tag>
</facelet-taglib>
```

Next we register this tag library file in `web.xml` so we can use it to add new states on the fly:

```
<context-param>
<param-name>javax.faces.FACELETS_LIBRARIES</param-name>
<param-value>/WEB-INF/mycompany.taglib.xml</param-value>
</context-param>
```

Shows page

PrimeFaces includes a full-featured calendar component that makes it easy to add scheduling to our web application. Let's look at how we can use the PrimeFaces `schedule` component to implement the **Shows** tab of our members' page.

This component has a simple API for adding events to the calendar that supports lazy loading for optimal performance while handling large data sets. It features a month view, week view, and day view, and has an intuitive user interface that supports drag-and-drop.

Let's get started with the `schedule` component. First we add the PrimeFaces tag to our JSF page, bind it to a `ScheduleModel` in our backing bean, and register some listeners for Ajax events.

```
<p:schedule value="#{eventController.userScheduleModel}"
id="schedule" >
<p:ajax event="dateSelect"
        listener="#{eventController.dateSelected}"
        update=":addShowDialogForm"
        oncomplete="addShowDialogWidget.show()" />
<p:ajax event="eventSelect"
```

```
           listener="#{eventController.eventSelected}"
update=":addShowDialogForm"
           oncomplete="addShowDialogWidget.show()" />
<p:ajax event="eventMove"
listener="#{eventController.eventMoved}"
           update="scheduleMessages" />
<p:ajax event="eventResize"
           listener="#{eventController.eventResized}"
           update="scheduleMessages" />
</p:schedule>
```

Following is a UML diagram that shows the classes involved in this example. The EventController class has listeners for different user interface events in the calendar, for example, eventSelected(), dateSelected(), eventMoved(), and eventResized(). This class is a @ViewScoped JSF managed bean and has a dependency on the CDI-managed @Stateless EventService class. It also has references to classes in our JPA domain model, in particular Event, User, EventType, and EventAttendance.

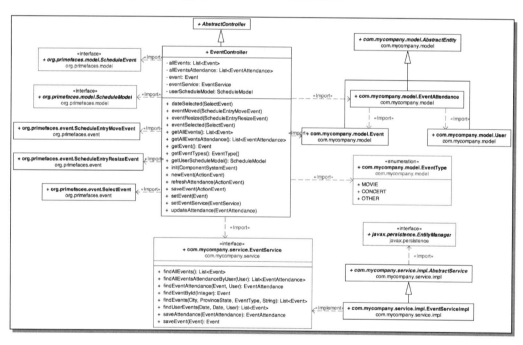

Rather than loading all calendar data at once, we can load a smaller set of events for the current timeframe, for example, one month, one week, or one day at a time. The PrimeFaces LazyScheduleModel class has a loadEvents() method that takes a start date and end date. We can override this method to execute a database query that loads only the data for the current calendar view. The following example demonstrates lazy loading:

```
public ScheduleModel getUserScheduleModel() {
    if (userScheduleModel == null) {
```

```
userScheduleModel = new LazyScheduleModel() {

    @Override
    public void loadEvents(Date start, Date end) {
        clear();
        List<Event> events = findUserEvents(start, end);
        for (Event event : events) {
            String title = event.getTitle();
            Date startDate = event.getStartDate();
            Date endDate = event.getEndDate();
            addEvent(new DefaultScheduleEvent(title,
            startDate, endDate, event));
        }
    }
};
}
return userScheduleModel;
}
```

Reviews page

This screenshot shows the PrimeFaces `dataGrid` component in action. This highly flexible component can render a grid of rows and columns with pagination.

The reviews tab enables the user to give feedback about events they have attended. We use the PrimeFaces `dataGrid` component to iterate the events, and we render a paginator so the user can view several pages of events easily. On this screen the user can also toggle a yes/no button to indicate attendance, and rate an event on a scale of zero to five stars. These two features are implemented using the PrimeFaces `selectOneButton` and `rating` components. Please see the Javadoc comments in the source code of the `EventController` class for more details on this example.

```
<p:dataGrid id="reviewsGrid" var="attendance"
            value="#{eventController.allEventsAttendance}"
            columns="3" rows="6" paginator="true"
            paginatorTemplate="{CurrentPageReport} {FirstPageLink}
{PreviousPageLink} {PageLinks} {NextPageLink} {LastPageLink}
{RowsPerPageDropdown}"
            rowsPerPageTemplate="9,12,15">
    . . .
<p:selectOneButton id="attended"
value="#{attendance.confirmed}">
<f:selectItem itemLabel="Yes" itemValue="true" />
<f:selectItem itemLabel="No" itemValue="false" />
<p:ajax update="@form"
listener="#{eventController.updateAttendance(attendance)}"
        process="@this" />
</p:selectOneButton>
<p:rating id="rating" value="#{attendance.rating}" stars="5"
          disabled="#{!attendance.confirmed}">
<p:ajax process="@this"
listener="#{eventController.updateAttendance(attendance)}" />
</p:rating>
    . . .
</p:dataGrid>
```

JSF2 composite component with PrimeFaces

The **Contacts** tab is where users can connect with their friends, family, and colleagues and chat online. For this screen let's write a JSF2 composite component that can render any list of `User` objects for desktop and mobile browsers.

In preceeding screenshot, we use a JSF2 composite component to render groups of contacts for the user. When a contact has signed in, his or her avatar image is highlighted to show presence. Clicking on a contact opens a live chat dialog that showcases the PrimeFaces Push technology.

We enable our JSF2 composite component to be integrated in a mobile UI based on PrimeFaces Mobile. In this mode, our component renders a simpler, mobile-friendly UI with some special CSS and JavaScript to leverage the PrimeFaces Mobile API.

Our contactList composite component has three attributes:

+ header: Specifies the text to be displayed above the contacts
+ value: Binds the component to any list of Userobjects
+ mobile: Set to true for mobile display mode

We can use our <mycompany:contactList>tag to display a list of friends, family, and colleagues. Notice that we use the PrimeFaces poll component to check every 10 seconds to see if one of our contacts has logged in.

```
<h:form id="contactsForm">
<p:poll update="contactsPanel" interval="10" />...
<p:accordionPanel id="contactsPanel" multiple="true">
<p:tab title="Friends">
<mycompany:contactList header="Friends"
value="#{contactsController.friends}" />
</p:tab>
```

```
    ...
    </p:accordionPanel>
    </h:form>
```

Let's see how we developed this component. First we declared the composite
component's interface:

```
<composite:interface>
<composite:attribute name="value" required="true" />
<composite:attribute name="header" required="false"
default="People" />
<composite:attribute name="mobile" required="false"
default="false" />
</composite:interface>
```

Next, we implement the composite component using the PrimeFaces `carousel` component
for desktop, and the simpler PrimeFaces `dataList` component for mobile. Notice that we use
the boolean `mobile` attribute declared in our component interface in our rendering logic by
using the `#{cc.attrs.mobile}` EL expression. If the `mobile` attribute is true, we render the
mobile UI, otherwise we show the desktop UI.

```
<composite:implementation>
<p:carousel style="width:100%" value="#{cc.attrs.value}"
            var="person" numVisible="4"
            rendered="#{not empty cc.attrs.value and not
cc.attrs.mobile}"
            itemStyleClass="person-item">
<f:facet name="header">
<h:outputText value="#{cc.attrs.header}" />
</f:facet>
<h:panelGrid columns="1" style="width:100%">
<p:commandLink value="Chat"
        onclick="chatDialogWidget.show()"
          update=":chatForm:chatPanel"
          actionListener="#{chatController.beginChat}"
        disabled="#{!userController.isUserPresent(person)}" />
<h:outputText value="#{person.firstName}" />
<p:graphicImage value="#{resource['images:user-icon.png']}"
        width="75"
rendered="#{userController.isUserPresent(person)}" />
<p:graphicImage value="#{resource['images:offline-user-
icon.png']}"width="75"
        rendered="#{!userController.isUserPresent(person)}" />
</h:panelGrid>
<f:facet name="footer">
<h:outputText value="Total: #{cc.attrs.value.size()}" />
</f:facet>
</p:carousel>
<!-- Mobile UI -->
```

```
<p:dataList style="width:110%" value="#{cc.attrs.value}"
             var="person" id="mobileContactList"
             rendered="#{not empty cc.attrs.value and
 cc.attrs.mobile}"
             itemStyleClass="mobile-person-item">
<f:attribute name="filter" value="true" />
<h:panelGroup
rendered="#{userController.isUserPresent(person)}">
<h:outputLink value="#chat" onclick="beginMobileChat()">
<p:graphicImage
value="#{resource['images:user-icon.png']}"
         width="50"
         style="text-align:left; vertical-align:middle;
margin-top:15px" />
<h:outputText value="#{person.firstName}"
         style="display:block; margin-top:18px;
font-size:0.9em" />
</h:outputLink>
</h:panelGroup>
<h:panelGroup
rendered="#{!userController.isUserPresent(person)}">
<p:graphicImage value="#{resource['images:offline-user-
icon.png']}" width="50"
         style="text-align:left; vertical-align:middle;
margin-top:15px" />
<h:outputText value="#{person.firstName}"
             style="display:block; margin-top:18px;
font-size:0.9em" />
</h:panelGroup>
</p:dataList>
</composite:implementation>
```

Chat feature with PrimeFaces Push

One of the most interesting features of PrimeFaces is the Prime Push API. Designed by Atmosphere Framework creator Jean-François Arcand, the Prime Push API supports asynchronous communication from the web server to the web browser on desktop or mobile using various transports such as WebSocket and Comet.

Prime Push technology opens up a whole new set of possibilities for web developers. We will implement a simple chat feature for our web application based on Prime Push.

What is WebSocket?

WebSocket is a standardized, full-duplex communication protocol based on TCP that can be used to establish a persistent, bidirectional communication channel between a web browser and a web server. WebSocket has better performance than Comet techniques such as long polling and HTTP streaming, and is well supported by modern browsers and application servers.

WebSocket support can be enabled in GlassFish 3 with a simple command:

```
$GLASSFISH_HOME/bin/asadmin set configs.config.server-config.network-
config.protocols.protocol.http-listener-1.http.websockets-support-
enabled=true
```

Once WebSocket support is enabled in GlassFish, we are ready to use Prime Push in our web application.

Chat room

Before we can see the power of Prime Push in action, we need to implement a chat room feature in our application. The PrimeFaces showcase application includes a chat room example, so we have adapted it for our purposes and integrated it into our application.

One of the coolest things about PrimeFaces is the ability to push updates to desktop and mobile users at the same time from the server using PrimeFaces Mobile and Prime Push technologies. The previous screenshot shows a live chat session in our web application between a mobile and desktop user.

Getting started with Prime Push

The first step in using Prime Push is configuring the Prime Push servlet in `web.xml`:

```
<servlet>
<servlet-name>PushServlet</servlet-name>
<servlet-class>org.primefaces.push.PushServlet</servlet-class>
<init-param>
<param-name>org.primefaces.push.rules</param-name>
<param-value>com.mycompany.websocket.DefaultPushRule</param-
value>
</init-param>
  ...
<load-on-startup>1</load-on-startup>
<async-supported>true</async-supported>
</servlet>
<servlet-mapping>
<servlet-name>PushServlet</servlet-name>
<url-pattern>/primepush/*</url-pattern>
</servlet-mapping>
```

An important point about this configuration is the use of a custom push rule implemented in the `com.mycompany.websocket.DefaultPushRule` class. This class provides some GlassFish-specific support that was necessary to ensure Prime Push worked properly on GlassFish.

Opening a WebSocket communication channel

The next step in using Prime Push is to establish the WebSocket communication channel between the web page and the web server. In our application, when the user clicks on the Chat link on the contact screen, we call the following method in our `ChatController` using Ajax to begin the chat:

```
public void beginChat() {
    User user = userController.getUser();
    RequestContext requestContext =
    RequestContext.getCurrentInstance();
    // ...
    requestContext.execute("socketWidget.connect(
    '/" + user.getUsername() + "')");
    pushContext.push(CHANNEL + "*", user.getUsername() +
    " joined the channel.");
}
```

Notice that we use the very cool PrimeFaces `RequestContext` API to invoke some JavaScript in the browser when the response is completed. We can do a lot more with the `RequestContext` API, such as update a DOM element, scroll to a component, and execute arbitrary JavaScript. Definitely check it out. Here we call `connect()` to tell the browser to listen for messages on the WebSocket communication channel.

Use of a PrimeFaces socket component

The PrimeFaces `socket` component establishes a WebSocket connection with the `PushServlet` running in our web application. Here it uses a communication channel named `/chat` for sending and receiving Push messages.

```
<p:socket onMessage="handleMessage" channel="/chat"
autoConnect="false"
            widgetVar="socketWidget" />
<script type="text/javascript">
  //<![CDATA[
function handleMessage(data) {

// append chat messages to output panel
var chatContent = $(PrimeFaces.escapeClientId('chatForm:chatPanel'));
chatContent.append(data + '<br />');

//keep scroll
chatContent.scrollTop(chatContent.height());
}
//]]>
</script>
```

When a chat message is received, our `handleMessage()` JavaScript function is called and the chat message is appended to the chat content panel.

Implementation of the chat room dialog for desktop web browsers

To provide a chat room user interface for desktop users, we implemented the following modal dialog using the PrimeFaces `dialog` component. It renders the list of active users on our website.

```
<p:dialog header="Chat" modal="true" showEffect="fade"
hideEffect="fade" widgetVar="chatDialogWidget" width="700"
position="center" appendToBody="false" height="400" draggable="true"
resizable="false"id="chatDialog">
...
<p:outputPanel id="chatPanel" layout="block"
styleClass="ui-corner-all ui-widget-content chatlogs"/>
<p:dataList id="users" var="user" value="#{activeUsers}"
```

```
                    styleClass="usersList">
<f:facet name="header">  Users</f:facet>
        #{user.username}
</p:dataList>
```

Next, we need to provide an input field for users to enter a chat message.

```
<p:inputText value="#{chatController.globalMessage}"
styleClass="messageInput" style="width:300px" />
<p:spacer width="5" />
<p:commandButton value="Send"
actionListener="#{chatController.sendGlobal}"
oncomplete="$('.messageInput').val('').focus()"/>

  ...
<p:commandButton value="Close" style="margin-top:20px"
actionListener="#{chatController.endChat}"
    onclick="chatDialogWidget.hide()"
global="false" />
```

When the user clicks on the **Send** button, the chat message text is submitted using Ajax and our `ChatController.sendGlobal()` method is invoked to push the message to the WebSocket channel.

```
private static final String CHANNEL = "/chat/";

public void sendGlobal() {
    String username = getLoggedInUser().getUsername();
    pushContext.push(CHANNEL + "*", username + ": " + globalMessage);
}
```

On the client side, the browser will receive the message over the WebSocket channel and our `handleMessage()` JavaScript function will append the text to the chat panel. We will look at how to implement the chat room feature for mobile users later in this chapter.

Show Times page

One of the main features of our web application is a search screen where members can find entertaining events in their city. This screen uses a search interface and Google map component with overlays to display the events from the user's search.

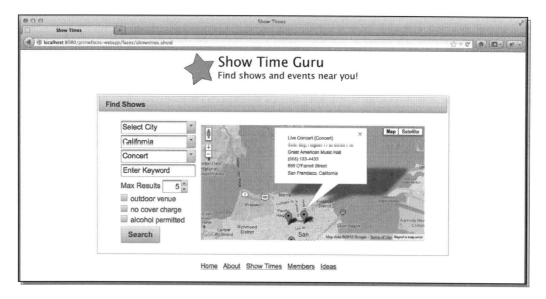

The ShowTimes page in our app uses the PrimeFaces Google Map component with overlays and markers to display search results to the user. This screen enables users to search for events in their city and find fun and interesting things to do.

Adding the Google Maps component

The Google Maps component is easy to use with PrimeFaces. In this code we use some EL expressions to dynamically control the map's center point and zoom level. The model attribute is bound to our search results model representing venues by their latitude and longitude coordinates on the map.

```
<p:gmap center="#{searchController.mapCenter}"
zoom="#{searchController.mapZoom}" type="ROADMAP"
id="showTimeMap" style="width:600px;height:300px"
model="#{searchController.searchResultsModel}">
<p:ajax event="overlaySelect"
        listener="#{searchController.eventSelected}" />
<p:gmapInfoWindow id="infoWindow">
<p:outputPanel ...>
<!-- Overlay content -->
</p:outputPanel>
</p:gmapInfoWindow>
</p:gmap>
```

Events search

In `SearchController`, our `search()` method starts by searching our database for events that match the user's criteria. If we find one or more events, we zoom in on that city; otherwise we show a map of the world.

```
public void search(ActionEvent evt) {

    // Get the list of shows from our database
    List<Event> events = findEvents();
    if (events.isEmpty()) {

        // zoom out to show world
        mapZoom = 2;
        return;

    }

    // reset center
    mapCenter = null;

    // zoom in to show city
    mapZoom = 12;
```

Next we iterate the events and lookup the map coordinates for each venue using the Google Maps web service API in our `getCoordinate()` method. We add a Marker object to our search results model to display an overlay about the event in the map. This overlay is shown when the user clicks on a map marker.

```
    // Build a model for the Google map
    for (Event event : events) {
        LatLng coords = getCoordinates(event.getVenue());
        if (coords == null) {
            logger.warn("Warning - no coordinates for location: "
            + event.getVenue().getCompleteAddress());
            continue;
        }
        searchResultsModel.addOverlay(new Marker(coords,
        event.getTitle(), event));
        // center map on city of first event
        if (mapCenter == null) {
            City eventCity = event.getVenue().getCity();
            mapCenter = eventCity.getLatitude() + ","
            + eventCity.getLongitude();
        }
    }
}
```

Mobile UI with PrimeFaces Mobile

PrimeFaces leverages the jQuery Mobile API to implement mobile web pages. Let's go through some of the screens in our application and implement mobile versions of these views.

Search page

The event search screen can be implemented for mobile easily using most of the same PrimeFaces components. The main difference is the use of the PrimeFaces mobile `view` component. This component has a `header` child component that includes the mobile navigation bar, and a `content` child component that defines the main content of this particular mobile view.

```
<pm:view id="main">
<pm:header title="Show Time Guru" swatch="b">
<pm:navBar>
<p:button value="Home" icon="home" href="#main"
                 styleClass="ui-btn-active"/>
<p:button value="Info" icon="info" href="#info" />
<p:button value="Login" icon="login" href="#login" />
</pm:navBar>
</pm:header>
<pm:content>

    . . .

<p:commandLink value="Join today!" action="pm:join"
        update=":signupForm"
      actionListener="#{signupController.createUser}" />
    . . .
<h:form>
<p:commandButton value="Search" update=":showTimeMap,@form"
          actionListener="#{searchController.search}" />
</h:form>
</pm:content>
</pm:view>
```

Login page

We will implement the mobile version of our web application using the PrimeFaces Mobile toolkit. This UI toolkit is based on jQuery Mobile and includes a number of JSF components to support rendering our views on a wide range of mobile platforms.

All the views of our mobile application are declared within a top-level `<pm:page>` container as a `<pm:view>` element with a child `<pm:content>` element. The following code implements our login screen. The entire mobile view will be contained in a PrimeFaces mobile page component using the `<pm:page>` tag. When the user logs in, we update this component after the Ajax request to render the logged in UI for the mobile user.

```
<pm:page title="Welcome" id="mobilePage">
...
<pm:view id="login">
<pm:header title="Login" swatch="b">
<f:facet name="left">
<p:button value="Back" icon="back"
 href="#main?reverse=true"/>
</f:facet>
</pm:header>
<pm:content>
<h:form id="loginForm">
<p:messages id="messages" showDetail="false"
 autoUpdate="true" />
<p:inputText id="username" label="Username: "
              value="#{credentials.username}" />
<p:outputLabel value="Password: " for="password" />
```

```
<p:password id="password" label="Password: "
                value="#{credentials.password}" />
<p:commandLink value="Forgot your password?" />
<p:commandButton value="Login" update=":mobilePage"
                    action="#{loginController.loginMobile}" />
</h:form>
</pm:content>
</pm:view>
...
</pm:page>
```

Member page

In the mobile members view, we use the PrimeFaces data list component to render a vertical list of links to navigate to the other views using GET-style mobile navigation.

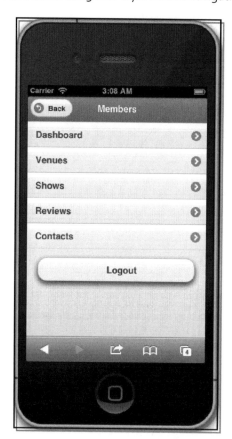

Notice that the header of this view includes a back button to navigate to the previous screen. By default, PrimeFaces mobile views use the slide effect to transition between views. Since the user is navigating back, we use the `reverse="true"` parameter in the PrimeFaces link to render the slide effect in reverse.

```
<pm:view id="members">
<pm:header title="Members" swatch="b">
<f:facet name="left">
<p:button value="Back" icon="back"
href="#main?reverse=true"/>
</f:facet>
</pm:header>
<pm:content rendered="#{loginController.loggedIn}">
<p:dataList>
<h:outputLink value="#dashboard">
        Dashboard
</h:outputLink>
<h:outputLink value="#venues">
        Venues
</h:outputLink>
<h:outputLink value="#shows">
        Shows
</h:outputLink>
<h:outputLink value="#reviews">
        Reviews
</h:outputLink>
<h:outputLink value="#contacts">
        Contacts
</h:outputLink>
</p:dataList>
<h:form id="mobileLogout">
<p:separator style="margin-bottom:20px;" />
<p:commandButton value="Logout"
                    update=":loginForm:username,:loginForm:passwo
rd"
                    action="#{loginController.logoutMobile}" />
</h:form>
</pm:content>
</pm:view>
```

Dashboard page

Our mobile dashboard view, like the desktop browser dashboard page, uses panels to implement the dashboard widgets. We make the panels collapsible so the user can expand and collapse them to use the available mobile screen space more efficiently.

This screen is implemented using the PrimeFaces feed reader component inside a panel component.

```
<pm:view id="dashboard">
<pm:header title="Dashboard" swatch="b"> ...   </pm:header>
<pm:content rendered="#{loginController.loggedIn}">
<h:outputText value="Welcome,
#{userController.user.firstName}" />
<p:panel id="entertainment" header="Entertainment"
            toggleable="true" closable="true" toggleSpeed="500"
            closeSpeed="500" widgetVar="entertainmentPanelWidget">
<p:feedReader
value="http://rss.news.yahoo.com/rss/entertainment"
var="feed"
```

```
                              size="1">
    <h:outputText value="#{feed.title}"
                            style="font-weight: bold; display:block"/>
    <h:outputText value="#{feed.description.value}"
                            escape="false"/>
    </p:feedReader>
    </p:panel>
        ...
    </pm:content>
    </pm:view>
```

Shows page

The mobile version of the shows screen also displays recent shows; however, we do not display the data in a calendar interface. Once again we use the PrimeFaces data list component to render panels for this view. Each panel displays information about the event.

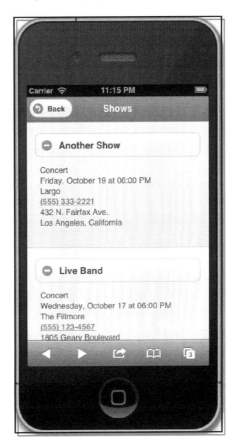

The following code shows the use of the PrimeFaces `<p:dataList>` component to render a list of shows in collapsible panels:

```
<pm:view id="shows">
<pm:header title="Shows" swatch="b">
<f:facet name="left">
<p:button value="Back" icon="back"
          href="#members?reverse=true"/>
</f:facet>
</pm:header>
<pm:content rendered="#{loginController.loggedIn}">
<p:dataList value="#{eventController.allEvents}"
id="eventList"
               var="event">
<p:panel header="#{event.title}">
<h:panelGroup style="font-size:1.2em">
<h:outputText value="#{event.eventType.label}" />
<h:outputText value="&#60;br /&#62;" escape="false" />
<h:outputText value="#{event.startDate}">
<f:convertDateTime pattern="EEEE, MMMM d 'at' hh:mm a" />
</h:outputText>
<h:outputText value="&#60;br /&#62;" escape="false" />
<h:outputText value="#{event.venue.name}" />
<h:outputText value="&#60;br /&#62;" escape="false" />
<h:outputText value="#{event.venue.phoneNumber}" />
<h:outputText value="&#60;br /&#62;" escape="false" />
<h:outputText value="#{event.venue.streetAddress}" />
<h:outputText value="&#60;br /&#62;" escape="false" />
<h:outputText value="#{event.venue.city.name},
#{event.venue.provinceState.name}" />
</h:panelGroup>
</p:panel>
</p:dataList>
</pm:content>
</pm:view>
```

Chat room for mobile devices

Finally, we display a similar contact page for mobile users. This implementation uses the PrimeFaces accordion panel component to render a tab for friends, family, and colleague contacts. We reuse our contact list JSF2 composite component to display the users for each section, except we pass `mobile="true"` to enable our mobile UI.

```
<pm:view id="contacts">
<pm:header title="Contacts" swatch="b">
<f:facet name="left">
<p:button value="Back" icon="back"
               href="#members?reverse=true"/>
</f:facet>
</pm:header>
```

```
<pm:content>
<h:form>
<p:accordionPanel id="contactsPanel">
<p:tab title="Friends">
<mycompany:contactList header="Friends" mobile="true"
                             value="#{contactsController.friends}"
/>
</p:tab>
<p:tab title="Family">
<mycompany:contactList header="Family" mobile="true"
                             value="#{contactsController.family}" />
</p:tab>
<p:tab title="Colleagues">
<mycompany:contactList header="Colleagues" mobile="true"
                             value="#{contactsController.
colleagues}" />
</p:tab>
</p:accordionPanel>
<p:remoteCommand name="beginMobileChat"
 actionListener="#{chatController.beginChat}"
oncomplete="clearChatWindow()"  />
</h:form>
</pm:content>
</pm:view>
```

We also set the filter attribute to `true` on the data list to display a text field for contact filtering. This feature enables the user to narrow the list using incremental search and is helpful when viewing a large number of contacts.

```
<p:dataList style="width:110%" value="#{cc.attrs.value}"
            var="person" id="mobileContactList" ...>
<f:attribute name="filter" value="true" />
...
</p:dataList>
```

It would be nice if our users could join the chat room from mobile devices too, so let's implement the chat room feature for mobile using Prime Mobile components. In this code, we used the PrimeFaces `remoteCommand` component to define a JavaScript function named `beginMobileChat()` that is called from our `<mycompany:contactList>` composite component when the mobile user touches a contact. This function sends an Ajax request to invoke our `ChatController.beginChat()` method to make the WebSocket connection and push a message to other chat users that someone is joining the channel.

```
<h:outputLink value="#chat" onclick="beginMobileChat()">
<p:graphicImage value="#{resource['images:user-icon.png']}"
                width="50"
                style="text-align:left; vertical-align:middle;
margin-top:15px" />
<h:outputText value="#{person.firstName}"
```

```
                                style="display:block; margin-top:18px; font-
    size:0.9em" />
    </h:outputLink>
```

Next, we define the chat view with a panel for the chat messages, a text field for input, and a button to send the messages. We use the PrimeFaces `socket` component to listen for Push messages.

```
    <pm:view id="chat">
    <h:form>
    <pm:header title="Chat" swatch="b">
    <f:facet name="left">
    <p:remoteCommand name="endMobileChat"
    actionListener="#{chatController.endChat}" />
    <p:button value="Back" icon="back" onclick "endMobileChat()"
    href="#contacts?reverse=true"/>
    </f:facet>
    </pm:header>
    </h:form>
    <pm:content>
    <h:form id="chatForm" style="text-align:center">
    <p:outputPanel id="container">
    <h:panelGroup>
    <p:outputPanel id="chatPanel" layout="block"
    style="width:100%;height:220px;overflow:auto; margin-
    top:10px;
     margin-bottom:10px" />
    <p:separator />
    <p:inputText value="#{chatController.globalMessage}"
    styleClass="messageInput" />
    <p:commandButton value="Send"
    actionListener="#{chatController.sendGlobal}"
    oncomplete="$('.messageInput').val('')" />
    </h:panelGroup>
    </p:outputPanel>
    </h:form>
    <p:socket onMessage="handleMessage" channel="/chat"
    autoConnect="false"
    widgetVar="socketWidget" />
    </pm:content>
    </pm:view>
```

That's it! Now users can join a chat from their desktop web browsers or mobile devices using PrimeFaces Ajax, PrimeFaces Mobile, and Prime Push technologies.

People and places you should get to know

One of the best things about PrimeFaces is the wealth of helpful information, sample code, documentation, and community support around this technology. This section includes references to some useful resources to help you get up to speed with PrimeFaces technology as quickly as possible.

Official sites

+ Homepage: `http://primefaces.org`
+ Manual and documentation: `http://primefaces.org/documentation.html`
+ Wiki: `https://code.google.com/p/primefaces/w/list`
+ Prime UI – Javascript widgetsbased on PrimeFaces JSF components: `http://www.primefaces.org/prime-ui/`
+ PrimeFaces Extensions – Community contributed extensions to PrimeFaces: `https://github.com/primefaces-extensions/`
+ Issue Tracker: `http://code.google.com/p/primefaces/issues/list`
+ Source code: `https://code.google.com/p/primefaces/source/browse/`

Articles and tutorials

+ Useful code nuggets and live demos: `http://www.primefaces.org/showcase`
+ Mock OS X Demo: `http://www.primefaces.org/showcase/ui/macosx.jsf`
+ Official source code for this book: `https://github.com/ianhlavats/primefaces-starter`
+ Courses and Learning: `http://primefaces.org/training.html`

Community

+ Forum: `http://forum.primefaces.org`
+ Blog: `http://blog.primefaces.org/`
+ PrimeFaces Tools for Dreamweaver: `http://www.jsftoolbox.com`

Twitter

+ Official PrimeFaces Twitter account: `https://twitter.com/primefaces`
+ Author's Twitter account: `https://twitter.com/ianhlavats`
+ For more Open Source information, follow Packt Publishing at the following link: `http://twitter.com/#!/packtopensource`

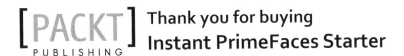

JSF 2.0 Cookbook: LITE

ISBN: 978-1-84969-162-8   Paperback: 112 pages

Converters, Validators, and Security

1. A collection of essential conversion, validation, and security recipes for JSF 2.0

2. Ideal for working with and processing web form data

3. All material presented in step-by-step recipes: find the one you need and implement it straight away – no need for background reading and theory

PrimeFaces Cookbook

ISBN: 978-1-84951-928-1   Paperback: 328 pages

Over 90 practical recipes to learn PrimeFaces – the rapidly evolving, leading JSF component suite

1. The first PrimeFaces book that concentrates on practical approaches rather than the theoretical ones

2. Readers will gain all the PrimeFaces insights required to complete their JSF projects successfully

3. Written in a clear, comprehensible style and addresses a wide audience on modern, trend-setting Java/JEE web development

Please check **www.PacktPub.com** for information on our titles

Made in the USA
San Bernardino, CA
23 December 2013